100 Lessons That I Learned In COLLEGE

What They Don't Tell You at Student Orientation

Cristina Doan

authorHOUSE®

AuthorHouse™
1663 Liberty Drive
Bloomington, IN 47403
www.authorhouse.com
Phone: 1-800-839-8640

First published by AuthorHouse 10/19/2009

ISBN: 978-1-4490-3750-5 (e)
ISBN: 978-1-4490-3752-9 (sc)

Library of Congress Control Number: 2009910634

Printed in the United States of America
Bloomington, Indiana

This book is printed on acid-free paper.

This book is dedicated to all those who supported me through the process of writing this book, and to every student about to embark on the most exciting experience of their life—college.

Lesson #1 That I Learned From College: Your roommate is not passed out drunk on someone's lawn from a post-game party if she is on Facebook in the morning.

Lesson #2 That I Learned From College: Pointing and laughing at people who are falling asleep in lectures prevents you from falling asleep yourself.

Lesson #3 That I Learned From College: Fire drills are utter chaos. Especially for the poor girl that was taking a shower when the fire alarm went off.

Lesson #4 That I Learned From College: Saving your water bottles and re-filling them from water fountains = best ghetto upgrade ever.

Lesson #5 That I Learned From College: Bring up "religion" in any class discussion and people start actin' a fool.

Lesson #6 That I Learned From College: Mandatory Alcohol Education online courses might as well have a video of a cult chanting "Alcohol is the devil" a million times. Regardless, people in college will still drink.

Lesson #7 That I Learned From College: Sitting in the front row in lectures means you'll be sitting next to the Suck-Up Club.

Lesson #8 That I Learned From College: Just because some people bring laptops to class doesn't mean they're good students. They're usually doing online shopping in class.

Lesson #9 That I Learned From College: People are really eager to get FreshMeat into clubs. So eager that they give you a million brochures about their clubs that you can either use as bookmarks or wipe your ass with.

Lesson #10 That I Learned From College: The reason why gym membership in college is so cheap is because you'll probably never go to the gym.

Lesson #11 That I Learned From College: The next time you look inside your wallet and all the money is gone, nobody stole it. You actually blew it all on food, clothes, and other useless crap.

Lesson #12 That I Learned From College: The only way you will wake up in class is if all your friends are laughing at how ridiculous you look when you fall asleep with your mouth open.

Lesson #13 That I Learned From College: When doing laundry, never leave your clothes unattended. By leaving your clothes unattended, your panties become prey to Mr. Pervert, and Mr. Lazy Cheap Ass will put his wet socks in your dryer.

Lesson #14 That I Learned From College: Always do reading for classes with a buddy. That way, if you fall asleep on your book, he or she will wake you up and you don't waste three hours in Dream Land.

Lesson #15 That I Learned From College: Once you start catching up in one class, you fail behind in another. I'm sorry, did I say "fail"? I meant fall. Fall behind. Right. Nobody is going to fail a class in college. (Insert sarcastic cough here).

Lesson #16 That I Learned From College: If you have an assignment that must be turned in via computer by a certain time, don't do it a half hour before it's due. Your computer might decide to freeze and watch you cry as your grade starts slipping through your fingers.

Lesson #17 That I Learned From College: When your college has a football game, never wear the other team's colors (intentionally or unintentionally). Unless you would like to get severely harrassed.

Lesson #18 That I Learned From College: Never shove your comforter, sheets, and all your other laundry in one dryer. Your clothes will have burn marks on them, and your beloved blanket will turn into Kentucky Fried Comforter.

Lesson #19 That I Learned From College: Walking in heeled boots on a hilly campus will scrape the skin off your feet, making showers excruciatingly painful. I mean, you **could** walk in boots on campus, but you'll be screaming instead of singing in the shower.

Lesson #20 That I Learned From College: If you run for any leadership positions on campus, no one really gives a crap what a pompous prick you were in high school. We don't care how many clubs you were president of in high school. People in college want to hear what you have to offer to certain clubs.

Lesson #21 That I Learned From College: Just because lingerie parties were cool in high school doesn't mean that they will be in college. Especially the first week of school. Inviting people to come into your room to dance in their underwear kind of freaks people out.

Lesson #22 That I Learned From College: Never leave your room with your Facebook account open. If you do, you will leave your poor Facebook account prey to friends who will change your status to, "Nick likes penis," "I am a lesbian," and other mortifying things that aren't true about you.

Lesson #23 That I Learned From College: In college, you will probably read more in one week than you read all year in high school.

Lesson #24 That I Learned From College: Plan something fun each weekend. Otherwise you'll be stuck in that jail cell called your "dorm" doing nothing on the weekends while everyone else is going to football games and doing fun activities for clubs.

Lesson #25 That I Learned From College: When you angrily slam your window shut after you've had it with the noise outside your dorm, make sure your thumb isn't in the way. Your thumb might turn purple afterwards and hurt like hell.

Lesson #26 That I Learned From College: Even though people are drunk at frat parties, they are at least sober enough to remember your name and add you on Facebook the next day.

Lesson #27 That I Learned From College: The irony of mandatory Alcohol Education online courses is that students usually complete them when they are drunk.

Lesson #28 That I Learned From College: The best way to learn the Greek alphabet is to go to multiple frat parties. (i.e. "Were you at Kappa Sigma last night?" "Nah, dude, I went to Kappa Delta Rho.")

Lesson #29 That I Learned From College: Don't wear anything too fancy to a frat party because drunk people will most likely spill their drinks all over you on the dancefloor.

Lesson #30 That I Learned From College: As crazy as it sounds, sometimes you wish your parents were there to yell at you to get your stuff done.

Lesson #31 That I Learned
From College: Make friends with
a domestic diva before you burn
yourself a million times with an iron.

Lesson #32 That I Learned From College: Whether you want to admit it or not, you will probably cry at least once because you miss your family. If not literally crying, then maybe just crying on the inside.

Lesson #33 That I Learned From College: There is always a token black guy in college. The one that is crazy drunk at frat parties and still has enough composition to pour you a drink is always entertaining.

Lesson #34 That I Learned From College: As much as we hate to admit it, food preferences in the cafeteria are dictated by race. (i.e. the Asians flood the stand handing out shiu mai and pork buns while the white kids avoid the curry chicken with rice).

Lesson #35 That I Learned From College: There are many clubs on campus that try to break racial stereotypes by having discussions on the topic of race. Regardless, the racist jokes persist after the discussions. (i.e. "What the hell is that Asian driver doing?" is usually said right when people start walking back to their dorms.)

Lesson #36 That I Learned From College: Snail mail from friends and family back home is cherished like never before in college.

Lesson #37 That I Learned From College: If you're a gay guy and good-looking, you're still going to have chicks drooling over you (even if you don't want them).

Lesson #38 That I Learned From College: If you're a girl, your bra serves as a key-and-ID-holder in lieu of a purse when you go out and party. After all, who wants to carry a purse when you're dancing?

Lesson #39 That I Learned From College: If you're going to use your bra as a purse, don't have a guy take it off when you're making out upstairs. Your keys and student ID will fall out and you'll be too drunk to notice.

Lesson #40 That I Learned From College: Never walk into the community bathroom showers barefoot, unless you want to feel other people's hair in between your toes.

Lesson #41 That I Learned From College: If you get text messages with scrambled letters, the senders are probably drunk.

Lesson #42 That I Learned From College: Your laptop will function doubly as your computer and your television, since you probably won't have room for a television in your tiny dorm.

Lesson #43 That I Learned From College: Even if you buy your books used, you will still drop a good several hundred dollars on books alone.

Lesson #44 That I Learned From College: If you have to walk a long way to class, listen to some good music on your iPod. It makes the trip so much faster.

Lesson #45 That I Learned From College: The loads of crap you brought to college that you thought you would need will probably be brought back home for Thanksgiving vacation.

Lesson #46 That I Learned From College: Don't get too excited when you get a letter in your mailbox. The letter will usually be from your loan officer, telling you that you will owe a castrating amount of money when you graduate.

Lesson #47 That I Learned From College: Co-ed bathrooms are scary at first. Mostly because you're not used to seeing people of the opposite sex in the bathroom. But when a male floormate walks out of the shower with a towel around his waist, showing off his abs...

Lesson #48 That I Learned From College: If a floormate goes to the bathroom and doesn't wash her hands afterwards, people will notice and not think highly of her.

Lesson #49 That I Learned From College: Just when you start loving a certain class and decide to major in whatever that class teaches, the class gets boring and you want to switch majors.

Lesson #50 That I Learned From College: Some clubs will require you to do humiliating things in order to get into the club. And sometimes, after you do those humiliating things, you won't even get into the club.

Lesson #51 That I Learned From College: Having a planner to organize your due dates is helpful, but it doesn't keep you from procrastinating on everything you have to do.

Lesson #52 That I Learned From College: Sunday is the worst day to plan a "cleanup" day with your roommates. Your roommates will either be hungover or finishing up the loads of homework they didn't do over the weekend. The whole "cleaning" thing gets thrown out the window.

Lesson #53 That I Learned From College: Whether people want to admit it or not, sororities never pick the chubby girl to be their sister.

Lesson #54 That I Learned From College: In college, there are more people out on the streets at night than in the morning. Usually, it's the other way around in normal places. You know, people crowd the streets in the morning to get to work and sleep at night? Yeah. Not in college.

Lesson #55 That I Learned From College: The kids who were president of every club in high school are the least active in clubs when they get to college. That's because they're actually in college now.

Lesson #56 That I Learned From College: The best place to sit in a lecture hall is in the back. You can see everyone who is asleep or on Facebook. Best yet, you can text your friends about how much you hate the class without getting caught.

Lesson #57 That I Learned From College: There will never be another time in your life when you will want the biggest stash of quarters possible. And I'm not talking quarters for gumballs. I'm talking quarters for all that stinkin' laundry you have to do.

Lesson #58 That I Learned From College: In high school, people strove for straight A's. In college, their expectations lower to a mere, "Holy crap, I hope I can pass my classes and not flunk out after getting wasted every night."

Lesson #59 That I Learned From College: Not all college dropouts are complete failures. They actually come back and help teach classes on campus.

Lesson #60 That I Learned From College: Never try to start a conversation in the bathroom when people are about to brush their teeth or use mouthwash. The conversation ends up like this: "So what are you majoring in?" (insert gurgle and spit noises here) "Rhetoric."

Lesson #61 That I Learned From College: Bringing nail polish that is your rival school's color is a bad idea. Especially if that's the only nail polish color you brought.

Lesson #62 That I Learned From College: If you meet someone at a frat party and that person is drunk, don't expect that person to remember you the next day.

Lesson #63 That I Learned From College: Residential Assistants get drunk too. And do embarrassing things that you wish you recorded on camera.

Lesson #64 That I Learned From College: Always have a snack and a drink with you. Vending machines are unreliable and are often there to take your money and **then** say "Out of Order."

Lesson #65 That I Learned From College: The saddest part of your day will probably be when you have to check your bank account.

Lesson #66 That I Learned From College: A friend in need is a friend indeed? Please. A friend who is motivated enough to walk a mile across campus to see you? Now that's a friend.

Lesson #67 That I Learned From College: If you don't think your major will make you a lot of money, don't fret. Start dating people in the Engineering Department. Yeah, they're usually ugly and awkward, but at least you won't starve in ten years.

Lesson #68 That I Learned From College: Always leave a frat party after being there for only a few hours. If you stay any longer, you give the cops time to bust the party.

Lesson #69 That I Learned From College: College is an opportunity to meet a lot of people. Too bad you won't remember half of their names.

Lesson #70 That I Learned From College: People actually eat cereal for dinner. They get sick of the generic crap served everyday at the cafeteria after a while.

Lesson #71 That I Learned From College: Even at one in the morning, you can hear people in the adjacent dorm cracking up at some stupid video online.

Lesson #72 That I Learned From College: Once you start baking cookies in the residence hall's oven, everyone wants to become your friend.

Lesson #73 That I Learned From College: Once there are sounds of loud moaning coming from a certain dorm, it becomes the "talk of the town" on your floor.

Lesson #74 That I Learned From College: There will always be that one student advocate who wants to implement change in a sea of students that don't really give a crap.

Lesson #75 That I Learned From College: College alumni are useful to a certain extent. You'll often find that they majored in something random and are now doing a retail job that they could have gotten without a degree anyway.

Lesson #76 That I Learned From College: Always choose your Monday classes in the afternoon. That way, you can stay up late Sunday night either partying or finishing up that paper due the next day.

Lesson #77 That I Learned From College: If you have a boyfriend in college, you are automatic "guy repellant." Meaning, all the guys asking you to be your "study buddy" will be disappointed once you say something like, "Oh, my boyfriend just texted me."

Lesson #78 That I Learned From College: Putting up a dry erase board outside on the door to your dorm invites very mature college students to draw penises all over it.

Lesson #79 That I Learned From College: Never friend your mom on Facebook unless you want her to stalk you constantly and know everything you're doing in college.

Lesson #80 That I Learned From College: Even though you're miles away from home, you still get a taste of the stupid drama you left behind via texts from jealous ex-boyfriends and phone calls from Mom about family problems.

Lesson #81 That I Learned From College: There is always that one student in your class who is way too old to be in college still. He or she tries to hang out with you and be hip, but something just screams "statutory" at the back of your head.

Lesson #82 That I Learned From College: No matter how nice you try to be to everyone in college, there is always that one jerk that you try to avoid but keep seeing everywhere anyway.

Lesson #83 That I Learned From College: International students make awesome drinking buddies. They will probably know more about drinking than you do, since they usually come from countries where the drinking age is much lower. Plus, who can resist a drunk, foreign accent?

Lesson #84 That I Learned From College: Just because you are away from high school doesn't mean that high school kids won't bug you about how to get into the college you got into. At least they'll believe anything you say about the college admissions process. (i.e. College Student: "Join every club that exists and kill yourself with hard classes." High School Student: "Okay!")

Lesson #85 That I Learned From College: Don't be ashamed to get a job where the most professional thing you'll say is, "Do you want fries with that?" That job may be the only job you can get.

Lesson #86 That I Learned From College: Playing "Apples to Apples" with floormates until 2 AM is fun until people start choosing "Star Fruit" as the winner card for an adjective like "Dangerous." Then you know the game is bull.

Lesson #87 That I Learned From College: In high school, sleep deprivation resulted from taking difficult classes. In college, sleep deprivation results from staying up all night doing stupid stuff on Facebook.

Lesson #88 That I Learned From College: You score brownie points when you say you support the gay community and you find out your teacher is gay.

Lesson #89 That I Learned From College: Some professors make six figures a year but still wear hideous clothing. Can't they afford anything more stylish?

Lesson #90 That I Learned From College: In high school, people woke up as early as 5 AM to get to school on time. In college, waking up at 9 AM is a challenge.

Lesson #91 That I Learned From College: When girls invite you to play "I Never" and/or "Truth or Truth" late at night, they are usually just doing it to find out if you're a virgin or not.

Lesson #92 That I Learned From College: Coffee kind of saves your life for one (and only one) lecture. This is because you get a caffeine crash right when you have to go to your next lecture.

Lesson #93 That I Learned From College: Making out with drunk people is gross because their breath usually stinks after they downed shot after shot of alcohol.

Lesson #94 That I Learned From College: Find out if you're a happy, sad, and/or angry drunk before you do something you regret (i.e. getting drunk and crying loudly in front of other people because you miss your mommy, etc.).

Lesson #95 That I Learned From College: When your folks come visit you at college, they usually ask, "Are those poor people hanging out at the park over there or students?" And that's when you answer, "What's the difference?"

Lesson #96 That I Learned From College: The best way to talk to a third roommate when the second one is sleeping is chatting with him/her on Facebook. The second roommate won't wake up.

Lesson #97 That I Learned From College: Ketchup and orange soda constitute your vegetable and fruit intake after a while.

Lesson #98 That I Learned From College: People steal forks from the cafeteria not because they need utensils, but because they need something to stop the doors to their dorms.

Lesson #99 That I Learned From College: The Residence Hall Association tries to put on activities so that you can get to know people in your building. The problem is, the activities are too stupid for anyone to want to attend them and then people on the same floor as you still don't know your name.

Lesson #100 That I Learned From College: Despite all the ups and downs, college will probably be the most exciting experience of your life.

Cristina Doan is a student at the University of California, Berkeley. She has received many accolades in writing contests around the Bay Area, such as First Place in NBC 11's and the Asian Pacific Fund's annual "Growing Up Asian In America" essay contest, finalist in the Martin Luther King, Jr. Essay Contest, and 2nd place in the Cesar Chavez Memorial Essay Contest. In high school, she was an Advanced Placement Scholar with Honor and scored among the highest in the nation in the Advanced Placement Literature and Composition Exam as well as in the Advanced Placement Language and Composition Exam. In addition to her ability to write well, Cristina Doan also has compassion for her community. In high school, she was a Distinguished Vice President of Key Club and also started a Peer Counseling club. Her dedication in these clubs caught the attention of Princeton University, who awarded her the Princeton Prize Certificate of Accomplishment for all the efforts she made to better her community. Cristina's experiences with helping others inspired her to write her humorous, witty book, ***100 Lessons That I Learned In College.*** She hopes that the lessons she learned in college will help other college students around the nation get through their first years of college with a laugh. Cristina Doan is currently studying to become a college counselor and aspires to be the humorous hero that college students need to find direction in their academic career.